LIFT HIGH THE FLAME
VISIONS of LEE UNIVERSITY

Betty & Henry Smith

This copy of *Lift High the Flame* is presented with deep appreciation for your friendship and support of Lee University. As we enter our Second Century, we are grateful to you for sharing our vision and mission, and we look forward to a bright future together.

Paul Conn

Lift High the Flame

VISIONS *of* LEE UNIVERSITY

EDITED BY
Jay Sheridan

PHOTOGRAPHY BY
PULITZER PRIZE-WINNING PHOTOGRAPHER
Robin Hood

Grandin Hood Publishers

LIFT HIGH THE FLAME:
Visions of Lee University

Copyright © 2018 by Grandin Hood Publishers and Lee University. Original photography copyright © 2018 by the individual photographers. Text copyright © 2018 by Jay Sheridan.

All rights reserved. No part of this book may be reproduced in any form or by any electronic or mechanical means, including retrieval systems, without permission in writing from the copyright holder, except in brief quotations or approved images used in a review.

Published by:
Grandin Hood Publishers
1101 West Main Street
Franklin, Tennessee 37064
www.grandinhood.com

Designed by Robertson Design
Franklin, Tennessee
www.robertsondesign.com

Printed in China through Four Colour Print Group, Louisville, Kentucky

Digital management and processing by Lauren Hood

ISBN: 978-0-9988056-7-2

This book is dedicated to
the Lee University Class of 2019 and beyond…
God has worked through thousands of people, over the span of one hundred years,
to provide the opportunity which lies before you.
So to the children of the Second Century, whether college seniors or yet unborn,
this book, this place, this Lee University is for you.

VISIONS *of* LEE UNIVERSITY

Contents

10	**Foreword** by Paul Conn
12	**The First Generation: 1918–1943** by Charles W. Conn
19	**The Second Generation: 1943–1968** by Charles W. Conn
26	**The Third Generation: 1968–1993** by Carolyn Dirksen
29	**Lee University at 100: 1993–2018** by Carolyn Dirksen
38	**Dr. Lois Beach**
40	**Global Perpectives** by Suzanne Holt
42	**Worship**
48	**A Heritage of Great Teaching** by Carolyn Dirksen
50	**100 Years of Athletics**
54	**Campus Life**
56	**Diversity** by John Coats
58	**Division of Adult Learning**
60	**Music**
62	**Service**
64	**Two Visionary Couples – One Wonderful Campus**
66	**Gallery**

Honor Roll

CENTENNIAL EXECUTIVE STEERING COMMITTEE

Jayson VanHook

Debbie Murray

Mike Hayes

Jerome Hammond

Cole Strong

Stephanie Taylor

Carolyn Dirksen

Jeff Salyer

Louis Morgan

Bill Green

Jean Eledge

Phil Cook

Erica Leggett

A CENTURY OF PRESIDENTS

A. J. Tomlinson – 1918-1922

Flavius J. Lee – 1922-1923

J. B. Ellis – 1923-1924

T. S. Payne – 1924-1930

J. H. Walker – 1930-1935, 1944-1945

Zeno C. Tharp – 1935-1944

E. L. Simmons – 1945-1948

J. Stewart Brinsfield – 1948-1950

John C. Jernigan – 1951-1952

R. Leonard Carroll – 1952-1957

Rufus L. Platt – 1957-1960

Ray H. Hughes – 1960-1966, 1982-1984

James A. Cross – 1966-1970

Charles W. Conn – 1970-1982

R. Lamar Vest – 1984-1986

Charles Paul Conn – 1986-present

CURRENT BOARD OF DIRECTORS

Dennis Livingston, Chair

Robert Daugherty II, Vice Chair

Marty Baker

Emmitt Beall

Patricia Carroll

Ishmael Charles

Hector Diaz

Bobby K Jones II

Wade Lombard

Jerry Madden

Byron Medlin

Jeff Robinson

Matthew Sharp

Lee Storms

Clayton Watson

H Bernard Dixon, Emeritus

David Ramirez*

Liaison from the Church of God Executive Committee

Acknowledgments

The publisher expresses a sincere appreciation to the numerous individuals at Lee University who have contributed tirelessly and with passion to this book by providing direction, leadership and research. Their limitless efforts and "Flame" made this book possible.

Foremost, deepest appreciation is extended to Brian Conn, Director of Public Relations, for lighting the way by sharing the Lee University Vision and Spirit, and for helping us to chart the course for successfully reaching our destination. We are also deeply indebted to Kendra Gray, Administrative Assistant to the Director of Public Relations, for her gracious demeanor while sourcing photographs, text and information in the most prodigious manner, and for being a most efficient traffic manager of communications as deadlines approached.

A special thanks is also given to Dr. Louis F. Morgan, Director of Library Services for Lee University Library, and to Dr. David G. Roebuck, Director and Church Historian for the Dixon Pentecostal Research Center, for sharing their vast knowledge of Lee University history and for providing many of the archival photographs presented within these pages.

Several Lee University staff and student photographers contributed stunning images, which greatly enhanced the distinctive flavor of this book. Among those on whom the publisher wishes to pass accolades are: Regenia Collier, Jason Moore, Travis Sturgeon, Mike Wesson, Lee Media Services, Josh Roden, Zack Camp, Ivy McCosh, Riley Mattila, Randi Vasquez, Andrew Miller, James Mears, Nathan Bivens, Hannah Morgan, Chike Okwudiafor, Tucker Shope, Matthew Melton, Arlyne VanHook, Carrie Christmas Workman and the Athletic Department and the Office of Publications. A special thanks is also extended to Chattanooga photographer Med Dement.

And thank you finally to the entire Lee University student body and professors for being the most cheerful, accommodating and inspirational group our team has ever had the pleasure to encounter.

Foreword

BY PAUL CONN

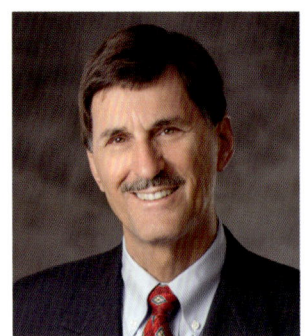

2019…2020…2021. Someday, those numbers will speak of the past. They will mark the earliest years of Lee University's second century. 2022…2025…2030. Those numbers will appear on the cornerstones of new buildings, on the covers of future *Vindaguas*, on the diplomas of thousands of graduates, some of whom have today not even been born yet. *If the Lord tarries*…We can take nothing for granted but if God is willing, future generations will look back at these dates as the beginning of our second century, our next hundred years.

But for now, locked as we are into our own histories, we think of 2018 as the conclusion of something, the end of the first hundred years. Only God Himself has the perspective to understand this moment of 2018 as the beginning of something new, a slight pause of celebration as Lee rolls into its second hundred years.

We call it our Centennial. We can look backward toward 1918 much more clearly than we can see the future. A wise person once observed that we live our lives in prospect, but understand them in retrospect. And that being true of individuals, it is even more true of institutions: we can see where we have been, even when we have no idea whatsoever where we are going.

So at our Centennial, at this grand benchmark of Lee University's life, we look back and celebrate one hundred years of God's favor. Hitherto hath the Lord brought us.

This book captures a glimpse of what Lee University is and what it has been during these hundred years. The story is one of constant change, beginning with a single small classroom, one teacher, and a dozen students, and evolving into a campus that stretches almost a mile through downtown Cleveland, with hundreds of faculty, thousands of students, and a complex network of programs and schools.

The *people* of Lee and the *places* they have lived are constantly changing.

People come and go. Students are at Lee for a few years, faculty and staff for a few years longer; whether it's the one-semester freshmen who have barely unpacked their suitcases or the legendary professors who spend their literal lifetimes at Lee, the people of Lee's hundred years have been a passing parade.

Presidents are only a small part of the parade, but their periods of leadership become the markers by which history is described. At Lee, presidential tenures have been conspicuously brief. Lee has had four presidencies that lasted only one year, and another three of only two years each. Among Lee's sixteen presidents, only two have stayed as long as ten years.

Faculty change too, but not nearly as often. In fact, there are fifty-two members of the current faculty and staff who have served more than twenty years.

The *places* which define Lee have changed over the years as well. The school started in Cleveland, Tennessee, where it stayed for twenty years before moving to Sevierville in 1938, staying there for nine years before returning to Cleveland.

The current campus has changed so dramatically that many alumni who visit after a ten- or fifteen-year absence find themselves in places they barely recognize. The footprint of the campus is six times the size of the original, and many buildings that held so many memories for generations past have been replaced with new, larger ones.

What has not changed at Lee, however, is the ideas. All colleges have a set of ideas which express their identity and drive their policies, and in most cases these ideas are expressed in the form of traditions or campus lore.

At Lee, however, our core ideas run deeper than mere traditions or educational values. Because they issue from our faith and our sense of God in our lives, they become spiritual commitments. Our enduring ideas about students, about learning, about destiny—they shape our life together and each of our individual definitions of sacred calling.

This is our culture. It's what makes Lee, Lee.

"The more things change, the more they stay the same."

That bit of wisdom was first offered in the 19th Century by a French writer, but it rings true when we think of Lee University in 2018. We look back into history, and we see ourselves; it's as if we are looking in a hundred-year-old mirror.

To be sure, much has changed. I stood on a commencement stage in May 2018 and looked out at an enormous crowd gathered on our new South Campus Quad. An excited crowd filled over five thousand folding chairs as the ceremony began. The faces of the graduates, as they marched across the stage in their caps and gowns, were projected on giant electronic screens, and the degrees they received were in such fields as political science, digital media, and nursing. Afterward, they scattered out over an expansive, beautiful campus while parents tweeted their pictures on cellphones and iPads.

It was a thoroughly modern Lee U moment—far removed from those stern images of Sister Nora Chambers with her little class of a dozen young ministers one hundred years ago.

And yet...*The more things change, the more they stay the same*. I stood on that stage and looked into the faces of all of those hundreds of 2018 graduates, and I saw the spiritual sons and daughters of Nora Chambers. No question about it. They have the same connection to Jesus Christ, the same sense of calling, the same courage and optimism about their future in a turbulent world.

And I looked out at the Lee faculty, resplendent in the bright colors of their academic profession, wearing regalia from the finest and most celebrated Ph.D. programs and graduate schools in the nation. A far cry from Sister Nora, whose diploma from a small Bible institute made her one of the best-educated ministers in the Church of God of her time.

And yet...I recognized Nora Chambers in this faculty of 2018. Like her, they are intelligent and strong. They care deeply. They have recognized that God can leverage their intellectual and spiritual gifts to shape the world for many years to come, just as He used Nora Chambers.

Lee has developed so impressively over the past quarter century that I am often asked to explain how it has all happened. What is different about Lee? Here is my answer: at Lee, we know who we are. We know to whom we belong. We know why we are here. Not to build great monuments to humankind, not to seek intellectual refinement, not just to grow and improve for the sake of success itself. We are here to prepare students to be servants of God in a complex, demanding world.

Our journey started one hundred years ago, and God willing, we are far from finished. In that humble classroom on a cold winter morning in 1918, Nora knew exactly what she was doing. She didn't know the shape of it, or the details, but she knew that it was God at work within her. *The more things change, the more they stay the same.*

THE STORY OF LEE UNIVERSITY:

The First Generation
1918–1943

BY CHARLES W. CONN

WRITTEN IN 1993

A BOLD PURPOSE

The Church of God began the school that would become Lee College as a practical way of training ministers. The move came at a time when some of its fellow Pentecostal bodies felt such an endeavor to be questionable and inadvisable. The church held a prevalent conviction that Jesus would soon return to the Earth, which put emphasis on the immediate rather than the distant future.

In 1911 the first effort was made to found a school for the training of workers. A committee of five ministers was appointed "to locate a place and erect a building for this school," and yet, seven years would pass before that desire was realized.

THE SHAKY BEGINNING

In November 1917, final plans were laid at the Church of God General Assembly: a school to be called Bible Training School (BTS) was instituted "for the training of young men and young women for efficient service on the field." The classes were to meet in the upstairs of the new publishing house in Cleveland. The first class of twelve students from four states met on January 1, 1918. Mrs. Nora I. Chambers, a lady evangelist and publishing house proofreader, was the only teacher.

It was a desperate time for the country and the church. World War I was being fought, and a deadly influenza epidemic gripped the entire country. It was a severe winter, and the accommodations were, at times, insufficient protection from the bitter cold. Half the students withdrew from the school, and only six stayed the course until the three-month term closed on April 5, 1918. One student died of influenza during the second three-month term.

The first class of Bible Training School was led by Nora Chambers, a lady evangelist who worked at the Church of God Publishing House, where the classes were held upstairs. Here, Church of God General Overseer A.J. Tomlinson (left) and Chambers discuss plans at the Council Meeting in November 1917.

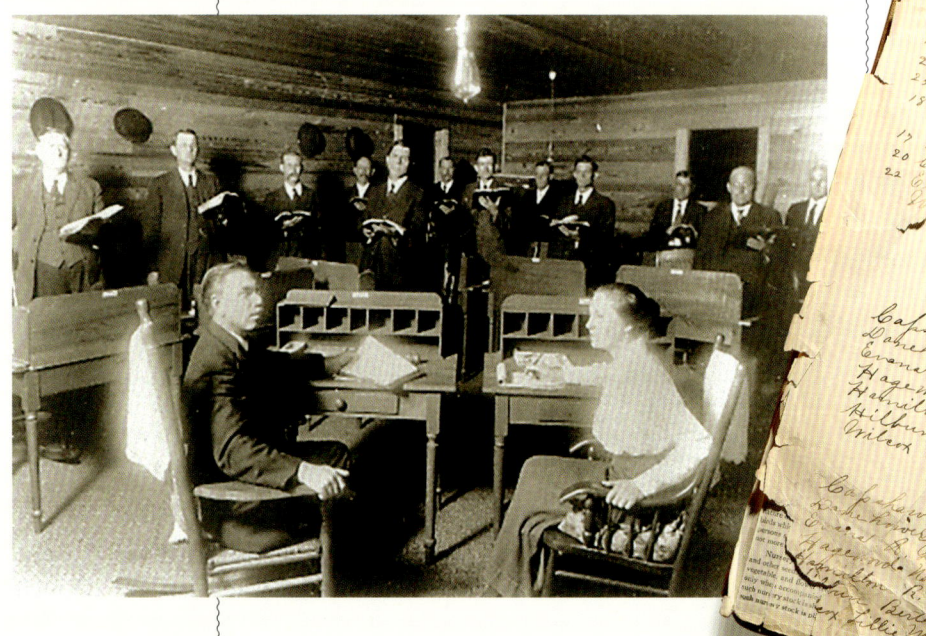

The first two graduates of the three-term BTS course, A.D. Evans and Earl Hamilton, were awarded diplomas.

When the fourth term began in September 1919, the deadly flu epidemic had passed and hopes for the fledgling school soared. A correspondence course was introduced for those who wanted to continue their education but were unable to come to Cleveland. It was an immediate success. Within one year, 788 persons enrolled as correspondence students.

Among the first class were both men and women. The youngest was Jessie Capshaw (left), 14, of Gaston, Georgia, the daughter of a Church of God pastor. She later ministered in Tennessee and Michigan.

Students shown in the photo above came from Georgia, Louisiana, North Carolina and Tennessee.

13

Tomlinson (below, top) served as BTS superintendent for the first four years, succeeded by F.J. Lee (bottom) in 1922 for one year. Under J.B. Ellis, the school moved from the small upstairs room of the Publishing House to the new Assembly Auditorium (shown opposite page).

THE EARLIEST LEADERS

The first superintendent of the Bible Training School was A.J. Tomlinson, general overseer of the Church of God. He was more than a titular leader because he gave active and capable guidance to the young institution.

Nora Chambers, the first teacher, was a woman of courage and ability, rare intelligence and considerable education. As a pioneer evangelist she had met and overcome many hardships. She worked for the Lord under physical duress and faced frequent threats of bodily harm or death. As a teacher, she imbued her students with the same sense of dedication and persistent effort in the face of obstacles.

Among her students were numerous persons who would later become distinguished in the work of the church, such as Paul H. Walker, John C. Jernigan, H.L. Chesser and Zeno C. Tharp.

In 1922, F.J. Lee became the superintendent, or president, of the school. That proved to be a blessing because Tomlinson departed from the Church of God in 1923 and new leadership salvaged the good work that had begun. When Lee was elected general overseer in 1923, J.B. Ellis was selected to head the school. Like Lee, he served the school for only one year. The school moved during Ellis's tenure from the publishing house to the newly constructed Assembly Auditorium. In 1924, T.S. Payne became BTS president, a post he would hold for six years.

VISIONS *of* LEE UNIVERSITY

Music has always played a central role in worship, and formal musical programs were added in the early 1930s to the curriculum.

A PROGRESSIVE ERA

From 1930 to 1934, the school took a decided upward turn. Under the leadership of its youthful president J.H. Walker, programs of music (under Otis McCoy), a high school division (under R.R. Walker), and commercial studies were added to the curricula. Enrollment rose from 87 to 131, with an additional 123 students in a short-term music institute. Walker remained at BTS until 1935, when he was elected, at age 35, general overseer of the Church of God.

LIFT HIGH THE FLAME

THE SPARTAN CODE

The life of the students was sturdy business in those days. The serious pursuit of learning was foremost and virtually altogether the activity of the student body. There was little or no provision for recreational and social interests. Some aspects of the rules and regulations would make today's students blanch in disbelief. There was simply no time for fun and games during that first generation of the school. Most of the students had to work at some job to help with their expenses. There was kitchen work, dormitory work, boiler room work, campus work and myriad others. Saturdays were usually given to some *en masse* project, such as cleaning the campus or repairing buildings.

There was little intermingling of the sexes. Girls had their part of the campus and boys had theirs. That usually carried over into seating assignments in classrooms, dining rooms, and worship services. Violators could expect to be chastened with demerits, which then had to be worked off. Of course, there were special occasions when fraternization was allowed—but all under the watchful eye of chaperones. Those cherished times were rare and well-anticipated Sunday afternoons or holidays. Still, romances did develop, and, as is attested by a generation of older alumni, many successful, happy marriages resulted.

Under J.H. Walker's leadership, total enrollment at the Bible Training School grew to nearly 250.

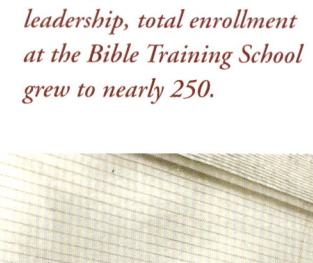

What students may have missed in social life was made up for in spiritual activity. Chapel services were almost daily, and there were conducted revivals, gospel music concerts, and all-night prayer meetings. The administration shared the needs of the school, spiritual and otherwise, with the students and sought their prayers and supplications. The Spartan way of life created a collegiality that was real and lasting.

YEARS OF CHALLENGE

The years 1935 to 1943 brought great opportunities to the school and led it to the threshold of respectability as a serious academic institution. Zeno C. Tharp, like Walker before him, was an alumnus of the school. Tharp was superintendent for nine years, 1935–44. He guided the school through years of financial difficulty and the restrictive days of World War II. Growth demanded larger facilities. This need was eased temporarily by the purchase of the old Murphy Collegiate Institute in the picturesque town of Sevierville, Tennessee, in 1938, and enrollment grew steadily past two hundred.

There was impressive physical expansion, but the greater growth was in academic mood and purpose. Dreams of accreditation were born, and the high school was accredited by the Southern Association of Colleges in 1941. BTS, which had been much like a cozy family of learners, now began a steady march toward becoming a college, and the erstwhile office of superintendent of education would become that of president. A long-dreamed-of student yearbook was finally launched in 1942, under the imposing name of *Vindagua*, which meant "window" or "place of vista."

In 1943, the first twenty-five years of the school ended on an optimistic level. Among the 450 students enrolled that year were many sons and daughters of those who had been there before them, and a full generation had passed through its halls.

In the years leading up to World War II, BTS flourished. Extracurricular opportunities such as choirs and performance groups emerged, and growth created the need to move to a new facility in Sevierville, Tennessee in 1938.

LIFT HIGH THE FLAME

Meanwhile, a correspondence learning program was introduced, which soon attracted hundreds of students who sought knowledge they could spread to their congregations and communities, across the country and around the world.

Bible Students' Motto: "A quitter never wins... a winner never quits."
Bible Verse Motto: Phil. 4:13, "I can do all things through Christ which strengtheneth me."

HOME STUDY BIBLE COURSES
BIBLE TRAINING SCHOOL
SEVIERVILLE, TENNESSEE

Dear Christian Friend,

We wish to acknowledge receipt of your remittance:

$ 1.50

We pray the Lord will repay you and bless you.

Avis Swiger
C. M. JENKERSON,
Instructor by Correspondence.

Do you know the Bible Training School's Home Study Department has students in practically every state in the United States and many distant lands? We are also sending free Bible Courses to prisoners by the free will offering plan. If you feel led to contribute to this worthy cause we will appreciate it. Will you pray a special prayer for these hungry students of the WORD? Pray for God to bless them in their studies so they can become more efficient workers in winning lost souls.

18

The Second Generation
1943–1968

BY CHARLES W. CONN

WRITTEN IN 1993

BETWEEN TWO WARS

The second twenty-five years of Lee College history was as successful as the first twenty-five had been tentative.

By 1943 the simplicity of an earlier time had given way to the complexities of the new. An unprecedented boon for military veterans who wanted an education came with the end of World War II: the G.I. Bill of Rights provided college grants for those who had been in the military service. This act moved college education from a privilege of the rich and gifted to an opportunity for ordinary, working-class would-be scholars. Lee College was poised for a remarkable advancement.

Leadership during the 1930s and '40s, from left (above): Zeno C. Tharp, J.H. Walker, E.L. Simmons, Earl M. Tapley

POST-WAR LEADERSHIP

Zeno C. Tharp, BTS president since 1935, continued at the post until 1944. After Tharp, the board named J.H. Walker president. Walker, who was elected Church of God General Overseer in 1935, had earlier served the school with distinction. It was hoped that he could resume the leadership he had once given; however, that was not the case in this instance.

Although student enrollment set a record of 630 in 1944–45, in the eyes of some, things had not gone well otherwise, and Walker's return to the school was terminated after only one year. It is with some irony that World War II ended that year, enhancing prospects for the school's future, and the General Assembly of 1945 convened on the BTS campus in Sevierville, Tennessee. Walker retired to a local pastorate.

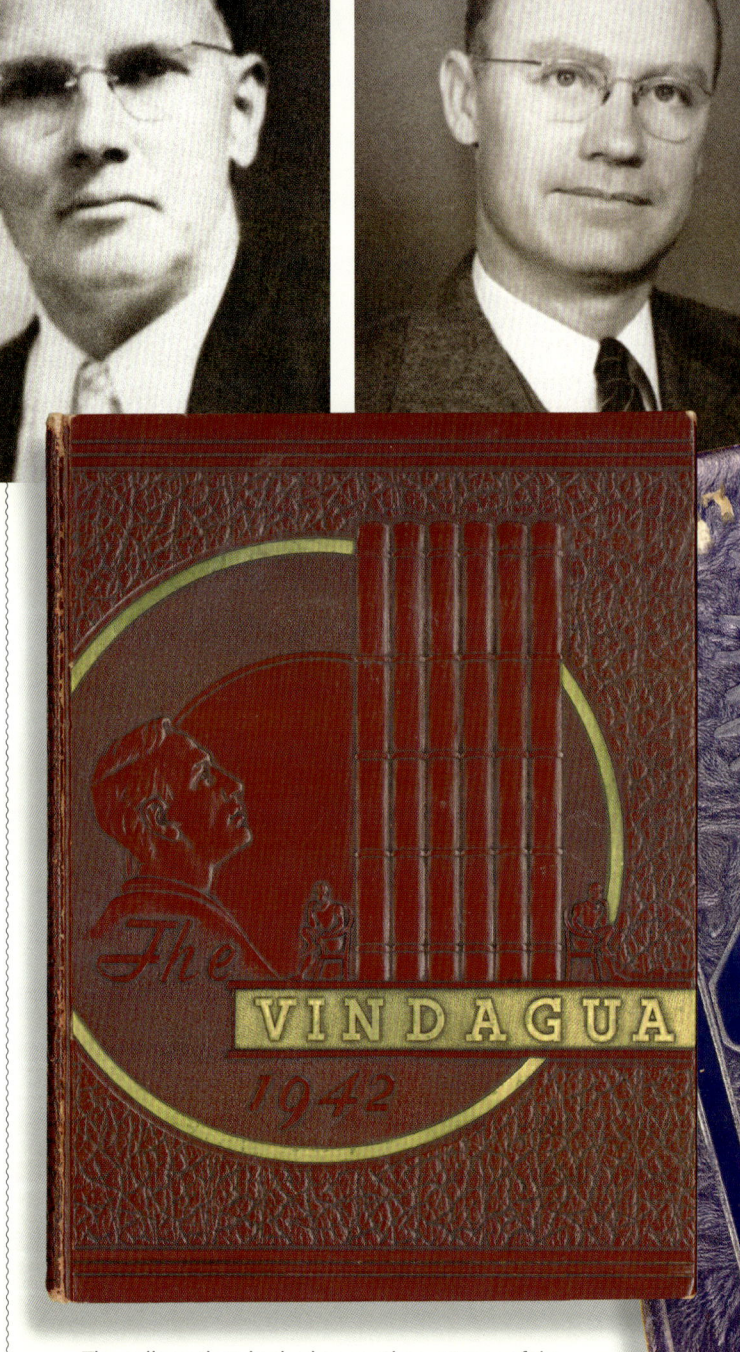

The college then looked to another veteran of the Church of God, E.L. Simmons, to lead it forward. Under his leadership there was notable property enlargement, with the completion of a new dormitory and extensive improvements of other facilities, and Earl M. Tapley, with degrees in education from Vanderbilt University and Peabody College, was named dean of the college.

VISIONS *of* LEE UNIVERSITY

A NEW CAMPUS, COLLEGE, AND NAME

Under the guidance of Simmons and Tapley, the school began to gain attention in the academic world. Graduates were soon able to transfer to major colleges for completion of their education. The eager stride toward accredited college status was quickened. And then, in 1946, a golden opportunity came to the Church of God: purchase of the Bob Jones College campus in Cleveland, Tennessee, which had been built originally as Centenary College, a Methodist institution. Occupancy of the campus meant that BTS would return to the place where it began in 1918, the headquarters city of the Church of God. The move was made in time for the 1947–48 school term, with the name of the school changed to Lee College in honor of its second president, Flavius J. Lee. President Simmons remained with the college only one year after the return to Cleveland, but the upward move in the field of education would continue.

The Sevierville campus of BTS (top left). In 1947, with the purchase of the Bob Jones College campus, the school returned to Cleveland with a new name, Lee College.

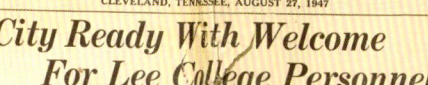

A GLIMPSE OF GREATNESS

In 1948, J. Stewart Brinsfield, a personable and progressive leader at age 35, was appointed president. In many ways his presidency was a herald of the future. He and Tapley formed a capable and compatible team, with the continued building of a competent faculty that included Hollis Gause, Mary Elizabeth Green, Robert Humbertson, and A.T. Humphries. Recruiters and music groups were sent out in an aggressive search for students and financial support. The "college spirit" was unmistakable on campus.

Off campus, there seemed to be a divided opinion about exactly what Lee College should be. Some felt that it should be a liberal arts college with a strong curriculum in theology and biblical studies, while others felt that it should strictly be a Bible college. A decade would pass before the matter was finally settled.

Lillian "White Corn" Little Soldier (pictured below) met Reinhold Klaudt during a revival service in the early 1920s and the two were later wed. This young couple was ordained into the ministry, and in the early 1930s attended Bible Training School in Sevierville, Tennessee. Born to Reinhold and Lillian were five children who were added to their singing and preaching ministry. The family traveled for over fifty years ministering known as the Klaudt Indian Family musicians. In the 1950s and '60s, the entire family attended Lee (and resided in Old Main) to further their education.

A TREADMILL DECADE

Although he was popular with faculty, students, and the public, Brinsfield was dismissed as president during the 1950–51 term. The change was followed by a period of frustration that saw the loss of Lee's recent gains, and the spread of a regrettable malaise. The loss of enthusiasm produced enrollment and financial problems that plagued the college through most of the 1950s.

Earl Tapley served as acting president for the remaining semester of Brinsfield's 1950–51 term, until the college board appointed John C. Jernigan president for the 1951–52 term. Jernigan served for only one year.

In 1952, R. Leonard Carroll, a South Carolina pastor, became president. His presidency was initially well received, yet a time of student decline commenced. By 1954, enrollment dropped to 530, which was 100 below that of 1944 when the school was still in Sevierville. And it would drop more.

Rufus L. Platt, dean of the junior college, was appointed president in 1957. Despite Platt's many efforts to stop the decline, it continued. College property was sold in order to pay its obligations. A sense of discouragement was perceptible in students and faculty. Some wondered, not always privately, if it could survive. Enrollment, down to 436 when Platt took office in 1957, dropped to 337 in the spring of 1960. Prospects for Lee College indeed seemed dim.

Several leaders attempted to reverse a downward trend through the 1950s; in spite of their efforts, the college gave up much of the growth of the previous two decades.

From 1960 to 1970, Ray H. Hughes and James A. Cross (above left to right, respectively) led the college through a period of resurgence. Donald S. Aultman (below right) was instrumental in the reorganization and accreditation gains made from 1968-1972.

THE END OF APATHY

An unprecedented thing happened in 1960. The Executive Council of the Church of God set aside an earlier decision of the board of directors and appointed Ray H. Hughes to be president of Lee College. Then, almost simultaneously, the Council called for a committee on Educational Aims and Accomplishments "to make a careful and comprehensive study of the entire educational program of the Church of God."

After suffering through a decade of decline, it seemed that the church was eager to roll up its collective sleeves in order to avoid such difficulties in the future. The committee, which included James A. Cross, chairman; Charles W. Conn, secretary; Ray H. Hughes, James L. Slay, and Lewis Willis, worked for two years, 1960–62, and produced the following recommendation: "it is our responsibility to sponsor one four-year liberal arts college, strong in education and the arts. It is our further responsibility to sponsor a strong school of theology and Christian training. We recommend that our efforts and attention be directed toward the full realization of such an institution, which is and shall be Lee College."

THE CLIMB RESUMES

President Hughes was best known as an evangelist, and for six years, 1960 to 1966, he led Lee College with a youthful zeal and evangelistic ardor. As Walker and Brinsfield had done before him, he gained the allegiance of the faculty and strongly identified with the students.

Several projects of campus enlargement improved school morale and confidence in the future. Among these were a modern administration building to replace Centenary's "Old Main" in 1963, and a science building in 1965.

Among efforts to stimulate enrollment, an annual "College Day" was initiated, when promising high school students were given a taste of college life. Enrollment thereupon rose remarkably to 629 in 1963, and up to 897 by 1966. A "President's Council" was created to encourage donors to support Lee College. The cumulative result of all this activity and energy was a renewal of enthusiasm toward it.

PASSING THE TORCH

When Hughes resigned from Lee in 1966, he was succeeded as president by James A. Cross, a church leader of tremendous influence and ability. Cross's appointment was an unexpected but popular one. A lifelong supporter of the college, he kept it on its positive course and led it to greater academic quality.

The faculty was notably enlarged during Cross's four-year tenure. Donald S. Aultman, as vice president and dean, merged the former separate colleges into one unified institution of three divisions: Arts and Sciences, Education, and Religion.

Probably the greatest achievement of Cross's years at Lee would come in 1969, with the college's accreditation as a four-year liberal arts college by the Southern Association of Colleges and Schools. It was fitting that, in 1968, President Cross led Lee College through its 50th anniversary celebration. The college was a mature and efficient extension of the dreams of half a century.

Images from Lee College in the '60s, including the auditorium (center), a hub of campus activity and the newly constructed Higginbotham Administration Building (bottom right).

The Third Generation
1968–1993

BY CAROLYN DIRKSEN

WRITTEN IN 1993

The dream of the Church of God denomination to sponsor a four-year liberal arts college was realized in 1967 when the Bible college and liberal arts junior college were merged, and upper-division programs were added in several disciplines. A new era of development began under President Charles W. Conn, who came to the office in 1970.

The first decade of Dr. Conn's presidency was one of comfortable prosperity. A gradual increase in enrollment was accompanied by an expanded academic program, upgrading of faculty credentials, and enhanced student services.

Campus facilities were improved under Conn's leadership with the addition of the 1,800-seat Conn Center, and Carroll Courts housing complex for married students.

In the late seventies, however, the college faced the problems of a decreasing pool of eighteen-year-olds. As the recession forced enrollment into a slump, costs skyrocketed, and by 1980, the college was operating with a deficit.

In 1982, Dr. Ray H. Hughes assumed the presidency for the second time, serving for two years. He continued Dr. Conn's efforts to solve the school's financial problems and refurbished aging facilities. Construction of the long-awaited Squires Library was begun in 1983. Despite Dr. Hughes's renewed focus on Christian service and denominational relations, the enrollment losses and sagging budgets continued.

The enrollment slide that began in 1979 began to turn under the leadership of Dr. Lamar Vest, who served as president from 1984–86. Enrollment had dipped to under 1,000 in the spring of 1983. Dr. Vest focused his attention on student recruitment and promotion within the church. Under his leadership, programs that had been discontinued during the retrenchment were reinstated, and new emphasis was placed on student life.

Working closely with Dr. Vest as vice president for institutional advancement was Dr. Paul Conn, who became president in 1986 and ushered in a renaissance. The fourth president in five years, Dr. Conn offered much-needed continuity, having served on the faculty for fifteen years prior to moving into administration. Growth in every area of the college can be documented over the first seven years of Dr. Conn's presidency. Under his leadership, enrollment climbed from 1,214 in 1986 to reach 2,000 five years later, breaking old records every year. An increasing number of the new students coming to Lee were academically talented, attracted by an enhanced scholarship program. As a result, the average ACT score for the freshman class increased substantially, and the larger student body became more heterogeneous in age and geographic and religious background.

A groundbreaking for Conn Center in 1976 attracted a crowd of church and community leaders (facing page). Following the two-year tenure of Lamar Vest (left), Paul Conn was installed as president (photo at right) by Board Chair Robert Fisher and Church of God General Overseer Raymond Crowley in 1986.

LIFT HIGH THE FLAME

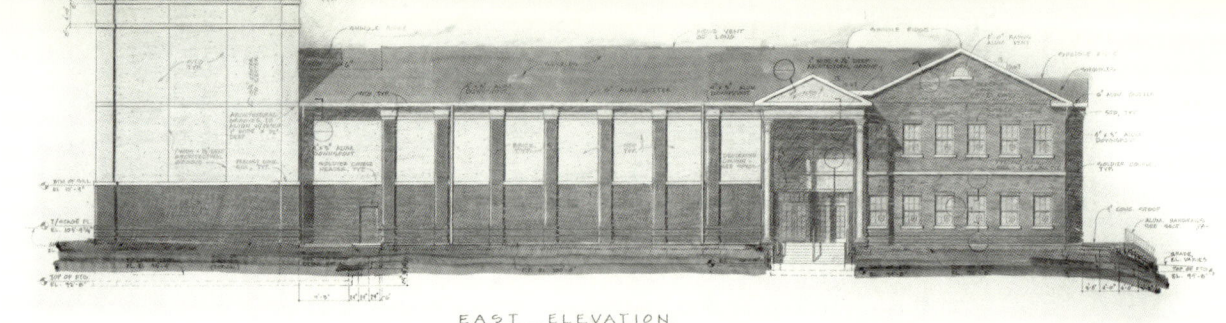

In 1992 Lee built and opened the Dixon Center, a 500-seat theater/recital hall and TV studio which expanded office, classroom, and performance space for the growing campus. Pictured on this page are various phases of the Dixon Center project.

Dramatic improvements in the physical plant kept pace with enrollment gains, with the renovation of the old library into the Vest academic building, the addition of three new dormitories (Davis, Sharp, and New Nora), the 500-seat Dixon Center theater/recital hall and TV studio, the DeVos Recreation Complex, Watkins office building, and a new maintenance facility. Significant renovation in almost every area greatly upgraded the working environment of the faculty and staff as well as the living environment of the student body. Two major capital campaigns ("Carry The Torch" and "Higher Ground") attracted several million dollars to the college and greatly expanded the base of donor support and expanded the endowment.

Increased enrollment and upgraded facilities made academic development possible, and several majors were added or enhanced as a result. A more appealing upper-division program also attracted well-qualified new faculty members with doctorates from well-known universities. Dr. Conn and the student life staff also focused considerable energy on campus spiritual life, enriching the chapel program and offering a wide variety of challenging speakers from diverse perspectives.

The face of Lee College changed dramatically under Dr. Conn's leadership, but its fundamental character and purposes remained unchanged.

28

VISIONS *of* LEE UNIVERSITY

Lee University at 100
1993–2018

BY CAROLYN DIRKSEN

WRITTEN IN 2018

In 1993, at its 75th birthday, Lee was poised for significant change. Paul Conn was in the eighth year of his presidency, and it was evident that his energy and vision were taking Lee to a place never before envisioned. The devastating Ellis Hall fire in November 1993 gave rise to a new surge of determination, and the new Atkins-Ellis Hall opened in fall 1994. More than just another dormitory, it was an embodiment of Genesis 50:20: "You intended to harm me, but God intended it all for good." Soon, enrollment topped 3,000, then 4,000, and records were broken with each new class, increasing the student population by more than 10 percent per year. Lee also successfully completed another review by the Southern Association of Colleges and Schools, putting in place the foundation for the next round of academic expansion.

From that launching pad, Lee has experienced twenty-five years of unimaginable growth and development, and at the century mark, the momentum had not slowed. To keep pace with rapidly increasing enrollment, Lee dedicated three new dormitories in the next three years along with the Curtsinger Music Building and the Deacon Jones Dining Hall. Recruitment accelerated with the addition of Voices of Lee, a premier a cappella vocal group, and Kingdom Players, a theatrical recruitment troupe. To care for the influx of new students, the Office of First-Year Programs, launched in 1996, created an award-winning strategy.

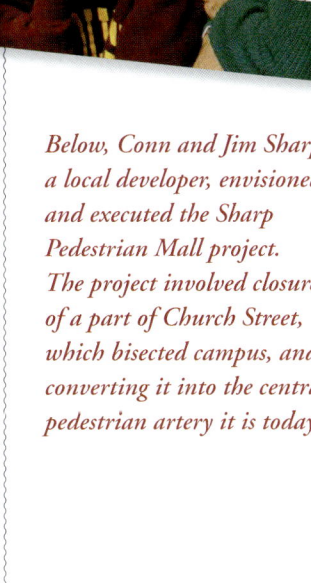

Below, Conn and Jim Sharp, a local developer, envisioned and executed the Sharp Pedestrian Mall project. The project involved closure of a part of Church Street, which bisected campus, and converting it into the central pedestrian artery it is today.

29

LIFT HIGH THE FLAME

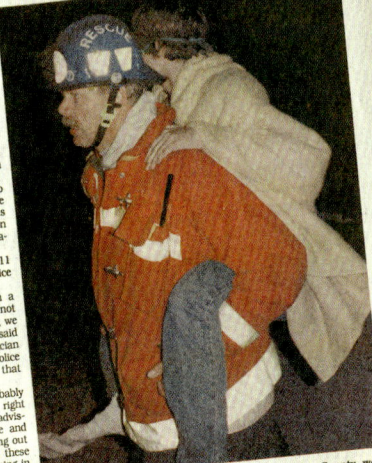

The Ellis Hall fire on November 4, 1993, was a defining event for the school. Seventy-six men escaped the dormitory fire with no loss of life, the building was a total loss, and a new Atkins-Ellis Hall took its place the next fall. Four young men who lived in a nearby neighborhood set the fire; they were later convicted of arson and served prison time for the crime.

VISIONS *of* LEE UNIVERSITY

31

LIFT HIGH THE FLAME

(top left) The newly expanded (1996) Deacon Jones Dining Hall, (above) Vice President Dale Goff oversees demolition on university property, (bottom left) an artist's rendering of the Curtsinger Music Building.

As students flooded in, the academic sector created meaningful new programs, and the mid-1990s saw some dramatic curricular changes. In 1995, the first graduate program, a master's in church music, opened the way for the development of programs across the disciplines. The faculty also approved a new general education core that included a required cross-cultural experience, taking most Lee students outside the United States to develop a more global perspective.

Behind the scenes in 1996–97, college administrators worked feverishly to prepare for a huge transition to university status. The eight academic departments were clustered into four colleges and schools, administrative offices were shuffled, and approval processes were realigned. Deans were selected, new stationery was printed, and new signs, banners, and marketing materials were created. Finally, after months of preparation, on May 10, 1997, Lee College became Lee University. On that single day, all signs on campus were switched, and Lee emerged into its new identity. It is hard to describe the heady atmosphere of those years when God's blessing was so immediately visible.

VISIONS *of* LEE UNIVERSITY

In the next decade, rapid campus development kept pace with unprecedented enrollment gains, and over the next three years, Lee dedicated the Helen DeVos College of Education, Keeble and Storms Residence Halls, and the Paul Conn Student Union. Lee entered the new millennium as a developing university with nationally recognized programs and an increasingly beautiful and functional campus. A world-class faculty had been drawn to Lee by its mission and by the energy, optimism, and faith that permeated the campus culture. By the end of this era, the percentage of faculty with doctorates had increased from 40 to 80 percent.

(top) In the summer of 1996 the campus played host to the Olympic Village for the whitewater events of the Atlanta Olympics. Lee alumnus Dewayne Knight helped carry the Olympic Torch to the venue. (center right) Board chair Darrell Rice cuts the ribbon on a newly constructed Humanities Center. (bottom) Board members Raymond Culpepper and Raymond Crowley enjoy the festive atmosphere of Celebration '96

During the early 2000s, Lee continued to add facilities that ultimately transformed the campus. The Humanities Center became a hub of activity on the north campus; the School of Religion drew students to the south. Lee acquired the nearby Mayfield Elementary School and converted it into a small village of programs. Lee also acquired the adjacent First Baptist Church property, opening the way for significant expansion to the south. In 2009 the Science and Math Complex (SMC) opened, more than three times the size of the Beach Science Building it replaced. One of the most distinctive buildings on the campus, dedicated in 2011, is The Chapel. A natural stone edifice with an imposing steeple, the chapel seats 350 and includes the Nichols Room and Courtyard.

The new Lee University School of Business is the latest major building added to the Lee campus in an aggressive expansion that has taken place over the last twenty-five years.

VISIONS *of* LEE UNIVERSITY

LIFT HIGH THE FLAME

The School of Nursing (open 2016) at dawn

VISIONS *of* LEE UNIVERSITY

Dr. Lois Beach

Lois Beach is one of the truly legendary teachers in Lee history. She joined the faculty in 1944, and taught continuously until her retirement as Professor of Chemistry in 1989. She was the first female department chair in Lee history, leading the Department of Natural Sciences and Mathematics for 23 years.

Under her leadership, and largely due to her vision and energy, this department produced hundreds of graduates who went on to professional and graduate schools and eventually to careers in medicine, research science, and many related fields. She was a fierce advocate for the natural sciences at Lee and was known for her gift of inspiring and encouraging her students to aspire greatly. Before her death in 2015, she saw the realization of two of her most cherished dreams: the construction of a new science/math complex, and the launching of a School of Nursing.

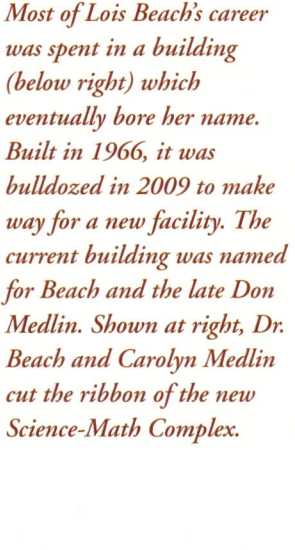

Most of Lois Beach's career was spent in a building (below right) which eventually bore her name. Built in 1966, it was bulldozed in 2009 to make way for a new facility. The current building was named for Beach and the late Don Medlin. Shown at right, Dr. Beach and Carolyn Medlin cut the ribbon of the new Science-Math Complex.

In 2013 the Tennessee State Board of Nursing gave Lee its first level of approval, and the university hired a director, enrolling the first class the next year. In 2016 the state-of-the-art School of Nursing building opened, and the first class of nurses graduated in 2017. The SON building created one side of a quad that took the Lee campus to downtown Cleveland for the first time. In addition to the School of Nursing, the South Quad includes a new Communication complex on Ocoee Street and the School of Business located in the dramatically rebuilt First Baptist Church education building. The former sanctuary is now Pangle Hall, a performance venue. A lacrosse field and the Forum, a multi-purpose tower built for the centennial year, completes the dramatic South Quad. Nearby, Dirksen Hall was opened in the fall of 2017.

In the final twenty-five years of its first century, Lee expanded from a 2,000-student undergraduate college to a 5,300-student university with flourishing programs and an enviable campus. Yet, despite all the dramatic changes and explosive growth, Lee at heart is still much the same place as it was when Nora Chambers welcomed the first twelve students. At the center of all Lee's work is still a deep love for the things of God and a deep longing to share that with students. Like Nora Chambers, Lee faculty welcome the unseen guest into every class meeting and dream of sending graduates out to make the world a better, more just and more merciful place.

An understanding of world cultures at Lee University dates back to the early days of the Bible Training School. A cross-cultural travel requirement formally instituted in 1996 has since taken students all over the globe, including Cambridge, England (right) in 2015.

Global Perpectives

BY SUZANNE HOLT

Encountering another culture and engaging with new ideas, values, language, and living standards remains among the most important education any human can receive. Just notice the intellectuals, scientists, theologians, and philosophers of the Western tradition whose contributions resulted from experience beyond the horizons of their own culture and country.

In 2005, the United States Senate passed a resolution declaring 2006 the "Year of Study Abroad." That same year (2005-2006), 732 Lee University students traveled and studied abroad, prompting the *Open Doors* report of the *Institute for International Education* to list Lee University as #1 in the United States for undergraduate participation in study abroad.

Lee's success was neither sudden nor was it a response to the US Senate's resolution but had deep roots in its missional DNA since BTS days when students felt the allure of travel for the sake of spreading the Gospel of Christ. This same spirit of mission later inspired students of Lee College who embraced summer travel with choirs, *Pioneers for Christ*, and medical missions teams.

The game changer for Lee University students came in 1996 when its revised general education requirements mandated cross-cultural travel for every student. This led to a new Global Perspectives program intentional about preparing students for cross-cultural encounters and the principles of faith integration upon return.

Study abroad on the surface can seem like a bundle of fun and unique experiences. Filing past tombs of Mao, Lenin, Ferdinand and Isabella, or the Poets Corner of Westminster Abby; praying at the Wailing Wall, Kings Chapel, or the Vatican; reflecting in wonder while visiting a diverse array of mosques, temples, and shrines; comparing degrees of material wealth in London and Paris with the staggering poverty of Garbage City in Cairo or the slums of Calcutta; student teaching among another people in places like Greece, Kenya, and Thailand;

doing language study in countries like Chile and France—as a rule, students returning from such encounters are more intellectually, spiritually, and even philosophically engaged, asking more serious questions about the meaning of life if not for clarity of vocation.

Study abroad is like a mirror reflecting the self as well as the heart of God. It seems a mantra to link Socrates with his famous admonition to know thyself, but Jesus taught us to identify first as children of the Father and members of his broader creation reflecting the *Imago Dei*. Drinking tea with the Atlas Berber of Morocco, comparing Hinduism, Islam, and Christianity in the twin-island nation of Trinidad and Tobago, grappling with the politics of apartheid in South Africa—these adventures and more have all helped Lee University students reflect on what such differences between themselves and others may teach them about the things that matter, whether of faith, knowledge, citizenship, vocation, culture, or family.

If they are fortunate, students will allow the images they see in the mirror of another people and culture to work a personal transformation in their lives. When completed sincerely and honestly with intentional reflection exercises, the Lee University study abroad experience continues to provide genuine value to the personal lives and vocational direction of students, the quality and engagement of campus culture, and the reinvigoration of civic life generally.

Even in a day when the costs of education are significant, we believe the value of this kind of experience is incalculable.

Other study abroad trips have included landmarks such as Machu Picchu, Peru (above) and the Great Wall of China.

Worship

The most important activity in the Lee experience is worship. From literally the first day of our existence, Lee students have come together to worship. The style of music and preaching are different, the venues have changed, but the core experience has not.

Worship during the BTS period was energetic, emotional, and evangelistic. A student in fall 1940 described it: *"The Friday service was one of our best ever. Each student brought the Spirit of God with him and we were blessed throughout the meeting. Brother Gosnell delivered the message. Christians were encouraged and sinners convicted. When the altar call was given, it was immediately filled. The Spirit descended as we sang, 'I Can Tell You the Time.' Oh, we had a glorious time, shouting, laughing, weeping, singing! Since opening day, we have had twelve saved, ten sanctified, and eight filled with the Holy Ghost."*

As BTS evolved into Lee College, now Lee University, student worship styles changed to reflect changes in the Church of God congregations they called home. That gradual reshaping of chapel continues to the present day. Worshippers in a Lee chapel are likely to find a style similar to their Pentecostal or evangelical churches back home.

The formula is the same after all these years: approximately one hour with lots of singing by the congregation, perhaps a bit of special music, then a full-length sermon. The preaching is usually done by guest speakers. Over the years, popular pastors have been the most frequent guests, and every generation had its favorites.

In the 1940s, James L. Slay was a regular guest. In the 1960s, Paul L. Walker filled the pulpit repeatedly. For a period beginning in the mid-1980s, Loran Livingston came to preach at least once each year for twenty-seven years in a row. Joe Novenson, a Presbyterian pastor from Lookout Mountain, Tennessee, was a perennial guest for almost two decades.

In earlier periods, chapel guests were likely to be white male preachers in the traditional mold. That has changed significantly, and the Lee pulpit is a more diverse place. Younger people, women, people of color, and speakers with ministries and experiences outside traditional pastorates are common today.

Some things have not changed: the emotional energy, the spiritual fervor, and the excitement of the music. In fact, for some students and staff who come to Lee from outside the Pentecostal tradition, their introduction to chapel Lee-style is almost overwhelming. One newcomer described it this way: *"I didn't know how they worshipped. So when I saw hands going up in chapel, the loud music, and the yelling (or what I thought was yelling), I panicked. But God wanted to teach me…"*

One tradition of Lee chapel which persisted throughout the 20th Century was the custom of a Sunday night service. In 1960, President Ray Hughes began the practice of preaching each Sunday night himself, and that established a pattern which continued for almost fifty years. It was considered part of the president's job description and ended only when the Sunday night service itself waned and instead a monthly "U-Church" (for "University Church") took its place. Today, with no Sunday service, the president still preaches ten to twelve times each year.

Another chapel tradition which still persists is that of Convocation – a special week of daily services each semester. Convocation has morphed somewhat over the years, but its powerful impact on students is as strong as ever. It was originally designed to match the model of summer camp meetings, with one guest speaker who preached every morning, and a different one each night — teaching in the morning; evangelism at night. Today, the Convocation pattern is six services in four days, with a different speaker at each service.

Lee still maintains what students call "required chapel." The requirement is not a popular idea to new students coming to Lee, evoking for many of them memories of their adolescent years, when they were hauled to church, voluntarily or not, by their devout parents. But after a few years at Lee, most alums look back on their chapel experience as something rich and memorable. It is the one time and place when most Lee students come together each week, and the experience for most students quickly becomes a positive part of their lives at Lee.

The possibility of eliminating the "required chapel" is often discussed, but no Lee president has ever seriously considered it. In the BTS years, chapel was held every day, six days a week. In the 1960s, the schedule shrank to four, then three weekdays plus Sunday night. Chapel now meets twice a week, on Tuesday and Thursday mornings, with Sunday night services once or twice a month. Students are required to attend two-thirds of the time.

With more students, the average chapel attendance has grown steadily, and today alternative venues are used to accommodate the large crowds. Students can choose between "big church" in the 1,800-seat Conn Center, a more sedate worship style in Dixon Center (500 seats), or a teaching or liturgical service in The Chapel, which can accommodate 350. Sometimes all three places host services simultaneously, and it is not unusual for any of these locations to be full at chapel time.

On the first day of the first year of Lee's existence, students joined together in worship. One hundred years later, and every year in between, the pattern has continued. Lee wouldn't be Lee without it.

LIFT HIGH THE FLAME

The Lee Choral Tradition

VISIONS *of* LEE UNIVERSITY

Choirs have been part of the Lee experience for almost a century. Here are pictured, from top left, clockwise: versions of the Lee Singers from the 1960s, three editions of the Voices of Lee, the Festival Choir singing at the 2013 Presidential Inauguration in D.C., and a choir specially assembled for an early Lee College Day recruitment event.

LIFT HIGH THE FLAME

The Forum Rises

46

VISIONS *of* LEE UNIVERSITY

When a new "South Campus" was developed on fifteen acres in the 2012-18 period, a massive bell-and-clock tower was designed to connect the new space with the core campus. Alumni of Delta Zeta Tau and Alpha Gamma Chi named the tower and surrounding plaza "The Forum" to signify a gathering place for all students.

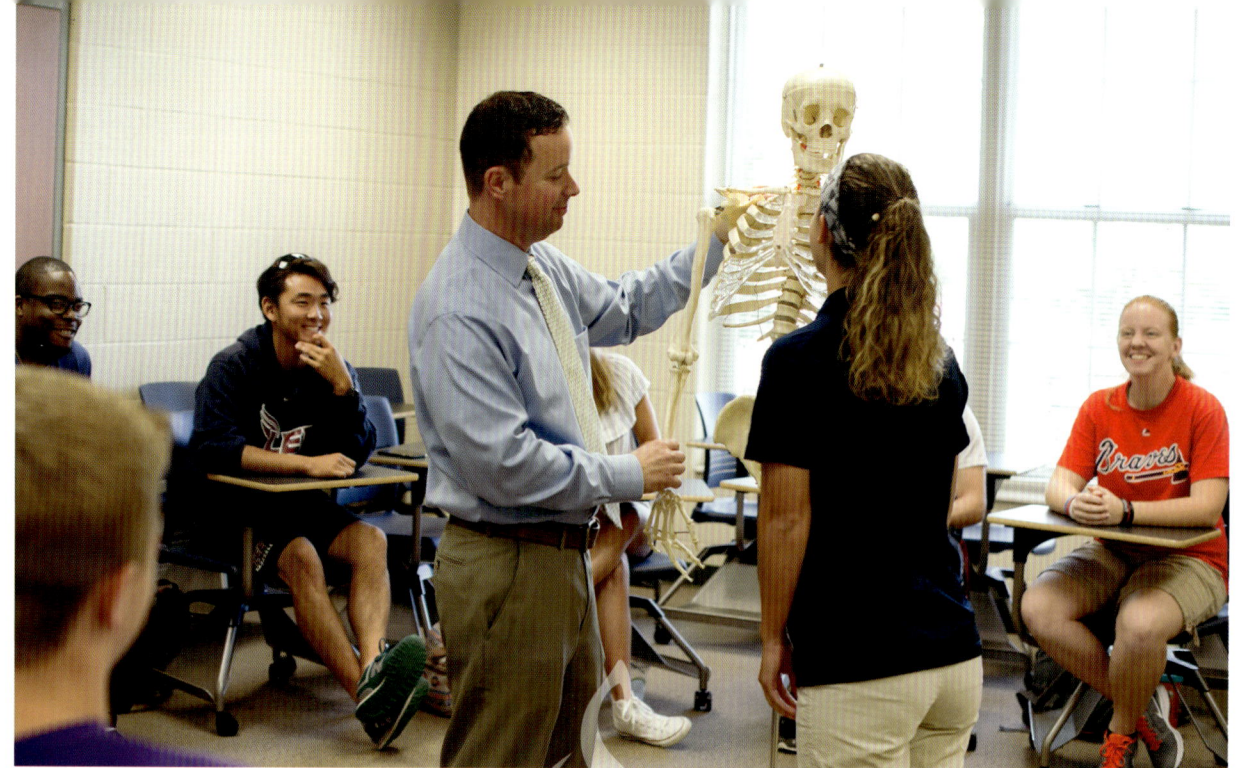

A Heritage of Great Teaching

BY CAROLYN DIRKSEN

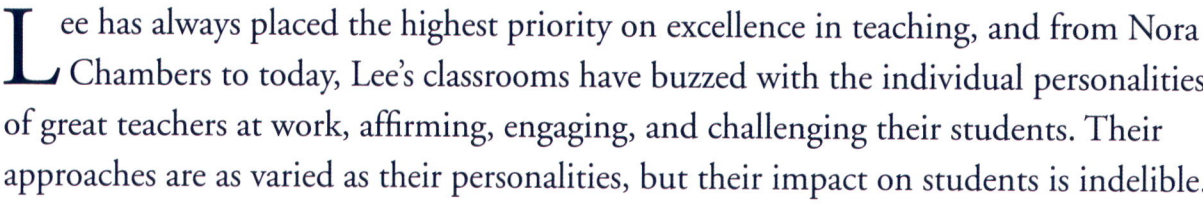

Lee has always placed the highest priority on excellence in teaching, and from Nora Chambers to today, Lee's classrooms have buzzed with the individual personalities of great teachers at work, affirming, engaging, and challenging their students. Their approaches are as varied as their personalities, but their impact on students is indelible.

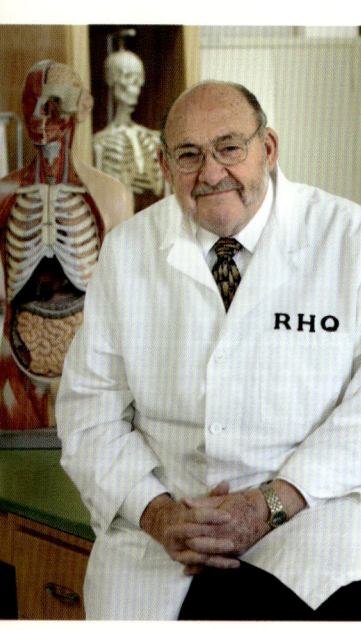

Don Bowdle, a professor of religion for more than fifty years (1962-2013) is the quintessential Lee faculty member, fulfilling the "sage on the stage" stereotype, eschewing technology and referring to group work as "pooled ignorance." He held to an absolute standard, impervious to students' appeals to curve the grades, yet his kindness, his gentle sense of humor, and his intellectual brilliance illuminated the classroom, and students flocked to his courses despite the difficulty.

Robert O'Bannon and Martin Baldree, represented very different perspectives on the age of the earth and the mechanics of creation, and their debate ignited student passions in their team-taught class, Science and the Bible. O'Bannon was a larger than life personality with strong opinions supported by research and deep knowledge of biology. Baldree was a brilliant Christian Education professor with equal verbal skills, a vast storehouse of knowledge, and great intellectual dexterity. These two giants went after the topic in front of a packed room of rapt students, and the sparks flew. Students learned both sides of the issue, but more importantly they learned that really good people with really good minds can disagree, argue passionately, and demonstrate both respect and affection.

Lois Beach owned the science department for decades, and her fierce dedication to her students is legendary still. Serving as the first department chair, Beach was passionate about sending graduates to medical school, and her chemistry classes were the crucible that prepared them. She set seemingly unattainable standards, but her confidence and pride in her students inspired them to achieve more than they thought possible, and dozens of them are now exceptional physicians. Penny Mauldin, Beach's protégé, returned as a teacher, and also mastered the profound balance of high expectations and strong affirmation. Mauldin succeeded Beach as chair, carrying on her tradition of excellence.

Delton Alford took the music faculty by storm, infusing the curriculum with a stronger strain of classical music, broadening the repertoire to include jazz, and converting the Touring Choir into the Lee Singers. As one of the first Lee professors with a doctorate, Alford raised the level in the classroom and on the podium, and lifted Lee's musical aspirations.

Now known almost exclusively as Lee's transformational president, Paul Conn was a classroom wizard whose mesmerized students converted in droves to the new psychology major. His classroom performance was a tour de force of flying chalk, portable rat labs, overturned desks, and the most full-on student engagement imaginable, all swirling around his astonishing verbal skills. In history, on a more reserved note, William Snell often strolled across campus dressed as Abraham Lincoln or George Washington, enlivening his American History lectures with period dress.

As a deep intellectual, Sabord Woods drew even reluctant students into the mysteries and magic of Shakespeare. One of his protégés, Susan Rogers, followed in his footsteps, completed a doctorate, and returned to Lee to light up the sky with her passion for the beauty and significance of literature. Their contemporary, Janet Rahamut, was a warm, accepting home for students on all sorts of margins. Through her deep affirmation, she drew them in intellectually and helped them see their own potential.

In many different ways across a variety of disciplines, Lee's faculty has demonstrated the kind of excellence that comes from being centered in a clear call from God to the classroom.

100 Years of Athletics

"Penalty kick," "Gulf South," "lacrosse," "D2." These phrases—never heard at Lee fifty years ago—are today essential elements of the athletic vocabulary of Lee.

Sports—the urge to compete physically—has always been a popular rival on college campuses with more intellectual types of comparison. The question of who is faster, stronger, more agile has been asked whenever and wherever young people gather, and those rivalries are a natural companion to the questions of who is smarter, more verbal, and better disciplined.

Sports and college students: it's a combination as natural as peanut butter and jelly.

In the first forty years of Lee's first century, sports was clearly pushed to the margins of campus life. It occurred naturally, informally, or not at all. Then gradually, as the school grew in other ways, the students' appetite for athletics became

VISIONS *of* LEE UNIVERSITY

appeal in the United States generally, much less in the South; baseball was regionally popular, but Lee owned no baseball field on campus.

The result was that basketball, softball and football dominated the intramural calendar, and those three sports were so popular that more than half the student body participated. The football played was, remarkably, not touch or flag football,

more obvious and the college responded in ways that were more obvious and better organized. Sports became a broadly based part of student life. Students expected athletic opportunities, both to compete and to watch, and administrators wouldn't disappoint them.

Most athletic programs at Lee, before the late 1940s, were recreational sports, loosely organized and connected either to physical education classes or to dormitory life. There was lots of activity, but the focus was on fun, rather than on setting records or traditional rivalries, and all of it "within the walls," in the classic definition of "intramural."

That growth of intramural sports accelerated with the move to the Cleveland campus in 1947. Golf was seen as an upper-middle-class luxury item, tennis was limited to a pair of deteriorating, cracked courts, and volleyball competed for space available in a single gym. Soccer had no popular

but full-contact tackle football with helmets and pads, which continued into the early 1960s when insurance concerns finally forced the school to adopt various tamer versions.

It is no surprise that at a school with rules against such popular entertainments as dancing and attending movie theatres, intramural sports were very popular from the 1950s through the 1980s.

Intercollegiate athletics were introduced in the early 1960s, with men's basketball only. A small group of Christ-centered colleges formed the National Christian College Athletic Association (NCCAA). In addition to Lee College, nearby schools such as Bryan College, Covenant College, Tennessee Temple University, and Trevecca Nazarene University were charter members of the organization who also formed a conference called the Southern Christian Athletic Conference.

That organization was Lee's athletic affiliation throughout the 1960s. Lee called its athletic teams the "Vikings" during those years and competed for numerous conference and athletic championships. Winning in the NCCAA became increasingly less satisfying, however, and Lee applied for membership in a higher-level organization, the National Association of Intercollegiate Athletics (NAIA), in 1975.

In 1982, Lee dropped the nickname "Vikings," in favor of the "Flames," which was a controversial decision for many alumni and students who had lived with the old mascot. During the same period of the early 1980s, when Lee's enrollment and budgets dropped, the school's athletic budgets were hardest hit. In an effort to expand beyond its basketball-only program, Lee had started "Vikings" teams with limited budgets and schedules in baseball, golf, cross-country, and tennis, but all those sports were eliminated in the lean years of 1980-84, and would never reappear in the Vikings era.

By 1984, only basketball and men's golf survived.

In the late 1980s, Lee committed to an athletic resurgence. Over a ten-year period, as an NAIA member, teams wearing the "Flames" logo appeared for the first time in volleyball, men's and women's soccer, women's fast-pitch softball, men's and women's cross-country, men's and women's tennis, and baseball was restarted. A few years later, men's and women's track/field began, and women's lacrosse was launched in 2017.

And the teams were good—especially Lee's women's teams. The school set a goal in the 1990s to make Lee a "magnet" for female athletes, and made a commitment to support women's athletic teams, scholarship for scholarship, dollar for dollar, at a level equal to their men's counterparts. The result has been a reputation for "Lady Flames" athletics which made Lee the #1 program for women's teams, across the board, in the Gulf South Conference in 2018.

Lee's women's soccer teams set an all-time NAIA record by winning four consecutive national championships from 2008 to 2011.

The Flames success in NAIA eventually led to the next step up. With Lee teams consistently so competitive in NAIA, the logical next step was to test ourselves in the National Collegiate Athletic Association (NCAA). So in 2012, Lee resigned from the NAIA and started a three-year trial period in NCAA Division II. In fall 2015, the process was complete, and the Flames became full-fledged members of the Gulf South Conference, a charter conference—and one of the most prestigious—in the NCAA.

Campus Life

One of the more subtle truths about higher education is the amount of transformative growth that occurs outside the classroom. When Lee students are not in class or chapel, and not out in the community or on the other side of the world, they must pull back into the day-to-day life of the campus and choose how they will engage. It is here in these moments where life lessons are learned, friendships are formed, and challenges are met and overcome.

It is here in the steady pulse of campus that we are forged. Do any of us who attended Lee have only memories of class and chapel? Not likely. If great teaching and powerful worship services are the bricks which build our Lee experience, the mortar that holds those bricks together is the flood of memories from campus, both mundane and momentous, that occurred elsewhere.

Who threw a Frisbee or football in Alumni Park? How many of us had a snack in the canteen, or met a close friend in the Viking's Den or the House? The Caf, the Ped Mall, the gazebo, PCSU are all shorthand names for places that became a part of "home" for many generations of Lee students.

And in these places, along with dorms and apartments, life occurred for us at a blinding pace, as we learned some of our first lessons in work-life balance. Should I do homework or go to tap night? Should I study for the test or wait until after my psychology club meeting? How many hours of sleep were given up to those time-management dilemmas?

It seems the typical college student has had this experience, and the Lee student is no exception. But though Lee University has always met freshmen at the door with a robust slate of extra-curricular activities, the menu is certainly growing with each passing year.

Student Leadership Council (SLC) boasts fifty events in the year on its calendar. That calendar includes some events like Parade of Favorites that have stood the test of time and some newer traditions, like Operation Christmas Child box packing party or Q Union.

There are over one hundred clubs, with about half of those being related to academics and the others organized around spiritual life, diversity, social service or justice. Students compete in thirty intramural and club sports, freshman Gateway instructors arrange several out-of-class activities, and each residence hall has individual meetings and a small group system for students to grow spiritually.

Dorm Wars is a perfect expression of Lee's abundant energy in campus life. The twenty-six-year-old event is a competition between dorms in various relay and timed events, the winner of which gets to choose a nonprofit to receive prize money. Each dorm raises awareness for its chosen charity and also vies for the bragging rights that go with the Dorm Wars title. This event packs the Paul Dana Walker Arena and gives each member of the on-campus community indelible memories to carry forever.

Whatever your passion was at Lee, missions or math or singing or softball, chances are most of your memories, even the tough ones, are of campus life, and even if the event or the club that hosted it wasn't of primary importance, it probably served as a backdrop for that memory, providing depth and color, making it last until today.

Diversity

BY JOHN COATS

Stepping on campus today, a visitor would find student, faculty, and staff from a wide range of backgrounds. Some of that diversity has always been a part of Lee, while other elements were added over time. When the Bible Training School (BTS) opened, its first generations of students might be what one would expect from a fledgling Pentecostal denomination in the foothills of the Appalachian Mountains—enthusiastic, young men and women from families with limited means and little experience with higher education. From that start, the school has moved toward an increasingly diverse population, drawing in students of different nations, races, denominations, cultures and classes.

At some schools' formative years, women had a marginal role; not so at Lee. From the very onset, the Bible Training School welcomed both men and women to its campus as students and faculty. Since the very first faculty member, Nora Chambers, and incoming class, women have earned a central place on Lee's campus.

It took longer for racial and cultural minorities to find their place at Lee. Many of the first people of color at Lee hailed from abroad, but especially from the West Indies. That international influence can be seen throughout the school's history, and today students hail from forty-eight countries across the globe. And, after the Civil Rights Movement broke laws that separated the races in the South, three African-American students desegregated Lee in 1966, pioneering the way for generations of students to come.

Both continuity and change can also be found when looking into the background of Lee's students. During the school's Bible Training School years (1918-1969), Lee's students were young, first-generation college students who often struggled to pay for school. Today, Lee serves primarily the traditional student, but also continues to embrace students who are underprepared for college. The university, however, has also welcomed an increasing number of non-traditional students. In the BTS years this was accomplished through correspondence classes. Today Lee reaches out to non-traditional students through the Department of Adult Learning's online degrees.

For many decades, Lee was a Church of God school, with its students, faculty, and staff drawn almost exclusively from its parent denomination. Lee welcomed students from outside the faith, but most were wary of the school's holiness Pentecostalism. Following the Second World War, an increasing number of non-Pentecostal students came to campus (some 25 percent by the late 1950s), but the school did not actively recruit outside the denomination until the presidency of Paul Conn.

Conn, while keeping Lee anchored in the Pentecostal faith, made the campus more broadly evangelical by welcoming both students and faculty from other Christian traditions.

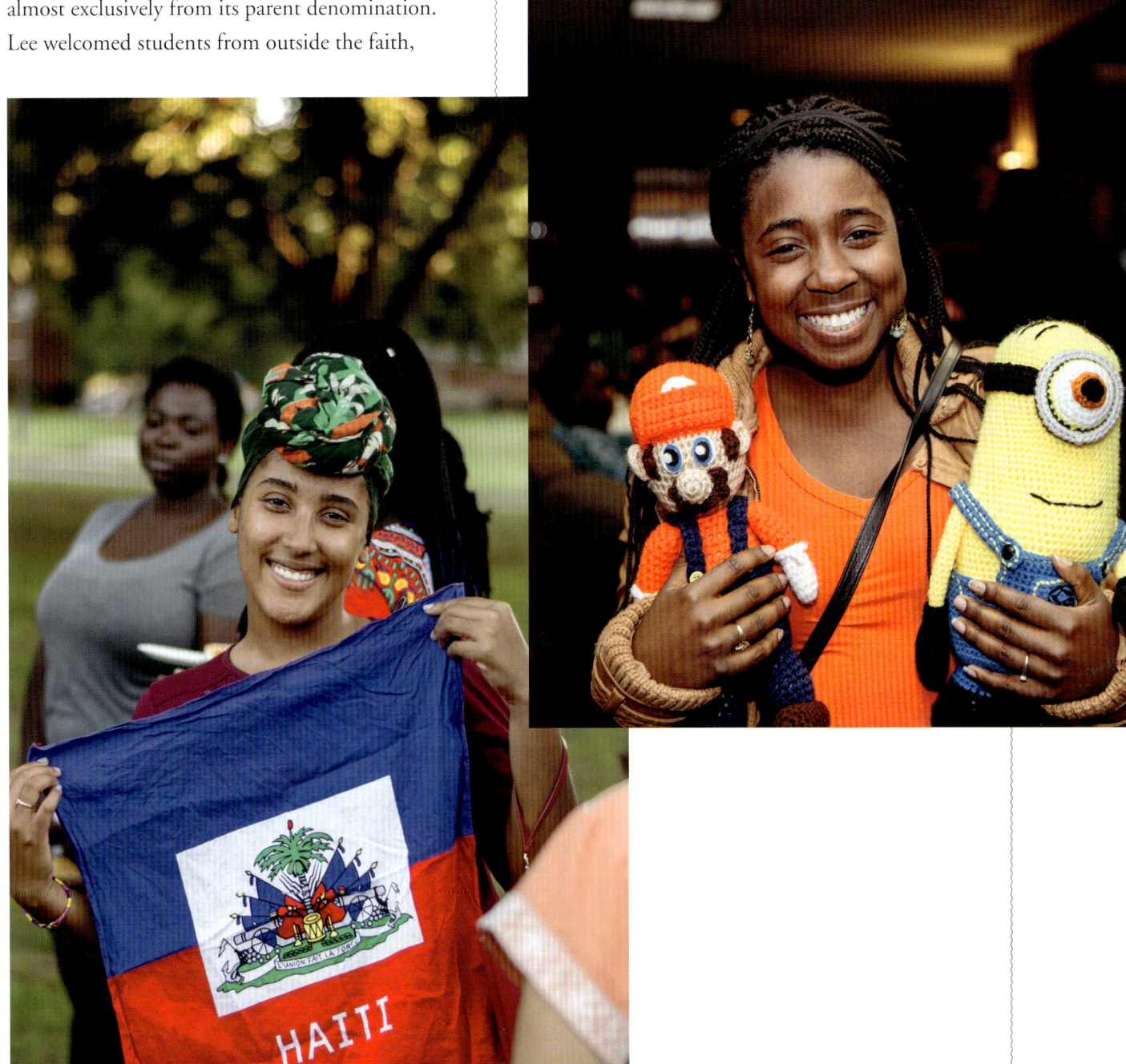

Division of Adult Learning

Nora Chambers' mission one hundred years ago was simple: use the Bible as the basis upon which to create better educated teachers, preachers and missionaries, who would then spread the Gospel far and wide. Within a year, Chambers' classroom was supplemented by a set of correspondence courses which served students who couldn't come to Cleveland.

With all of the modern advances of technology and transportation, the challenges related to continuing education have persisted: time, money, geography. That's why Lee University's Division of Adult Learning (DAL) was launched in 2014.

"Even when I was a student at Lee, when you felt called to the ministry it was as a preacher, and that has changed," says Dr. Jayson VanHook, vice president for information services at Lee and a key player in the DAL. "Now we have nurses, musicians, journalists and graphic designers who are seeking education that allow their lives and careers to become their own ministry."

The DAL was designed to address that overarching need to meet people where they are with opportunities for higher education: practicing ministers who never earned a degree, career professionals with an interest in ministerial education, emphases that focus on faith education and outreach, and then bachelor's and master's degrees in a range of areas spanning from criminal justice to music or business. And all of it is offered online.

Whether a student is interested in Christian studies—theology, children's and youth ministry, counseling, music and worship, among other focus areas—or liberal studies, behavioral and social sciences, or music education, the DAL provides distance education geared toward adults with a will to learn who are refocusing later in life, transitioning careers, or seeking to complete a degree they may have started years ago.

Master's degrees are offered in ministry studies, business administration, and marriage and family services. VanHook says it's a service that mirrors the Lee mission from its earliest days.

"We wanted to engage people in learning at all stages of life, and that's been an important part of who we are from the beginning," he says. "We wanted to provide an opportunity to experience Lee, even when they can't come to campus, and it's worked as we hoped it would."

Courses are discussion-based, and students watch lectures or read assigned texts before coming together online to engage in professor-led explorations of the concepts, engaging with each other in the process. Peer review and group work creates a dynamic that is unique from a traditional classroom, in that everyone has to be equally engaged.

In just a few years, enrollment has grown from about 250 students to nearly a thousand, and a new masters of music education was launched in the fall of 2018.

Most of the faculty are the same professors who teach every day on the Lee campus, and new instructors are thoughtfully immersed in the university's culture through professional and curricular development training. VanHook's information services team ensures that both the administrative and experiential components work as designed in a virtual environment.

"These are the same programs we offer on campus, from an academic standpoint, offered to students who otherwise might not have had the opportunity as a traditional college-aged student," he says. "Whether it's a police officer on a tight budget who works long hours or a minister who never finished a degree or a lifelong learner in a successful career, we believe this is an important component of our mission, to meet people where they are.

"I'm a product of Lee, and initially I was worried that this could somehow impact the traditional Lee experience. But I soon realized that more and more people from around the country now have a chance to feel what we have. That's what Lee was designed to do a century ago, and what our focus will continue to be for another century to come."

Music

Music performed from the heart touches the heart, and so much of the Pentecostal experience has been about the release of emotion, Lee University Dean of Music Dr. William Green explains. As a lifelong educator on the academic side of music, Green sees something special happening on Lee's campus, more so than on any other he's visited.

"I have professionals tell me all the time that these kids are different," he says. "Music is in the heart of God, and when you express that, it makes all the difference in the world. It has the ability to stir emotion, in the same way that people might see an opera and cry."

Early photos of students at Bible Training School show instruments prominently, demonstrating the significance that song has held from the beginning. That experience has evolved into a seriously acclaimed school of music, producing superb classical performers alongside vocal ensembles known worldwide for their powerful ability to captivate audiences with soul-soothing talent.

While about 300 Lee students might be music majors today, as many as 900 participate in ensembles each semester, ranging from Chorale directed by Dr. Green to the Lee Singers, founded by Dr. Delton Alford in 1963. For nearly a half century, Lee's traveling groups have spent many weekends on the road performing in high schools and churches, combining choral classics with the musical traditions of the denomination, gospel hymns and pop tunes.

Alford, who has studied the history of music in the Church of God, points out that a lot of early churches couldn't afford a fine piano or organ, so stringed instruments became central components in both worship and social engagement. Honing one's ability to play and sing well became another important way to glorify God, whether in the sanctuary or on the front porch.

Fast forward a hundred years, and the modern example of the power of the spirit in music might be best found in Voices of Lee, an a capella vocal ensemble that has been featured on television shows and stages across America. On the internet, their cover performance of the worship band Hillsong United's hit *What a Beautiful Name* went viral, approaching SIXTY MILLION views on YouTube as of this writing. Danny Murray, who founded and directs Voices of Lee, describes his mission succinctly.

"I'm trying to convince these 18- to 20-year-olds that they can look and act and perform like professionals, and we work every day, on the weekends, through the breaks, all summer long and on the road to do that," Murray says. "You teach them to harness their power and use it for good. They learn that they can marry their skill and hard work with the favor of God and the Holy Spirit, and that's where success comes from."

Now Lee is known as a 'dream school' for vocalists and musicians, as accomplished and credentialed as any larger music school in the country. Lee alumni are scattered throughout the who's who of popular music today, from Jay DeMarcus of Rascal Flatts to Clark Beckham of television's "American Idol" fame, and Jordan Smith, 2015 winner of NBC's "The Voice." Many who attended Lee have gone on to careers in classical music, and countless others have become teachers of music in universities and schools far and wide. Still others are simply using their talents shaped at Lee to bless their communities, congregations and families.

Most all of them first found their love of music in a small church somewhere, polishing God-given skills through practice and then finding the kind of emotion that touches the heart. Alford agrees, that's where excellence is found.

"A wonderful folk song performed artistically and authentically can be as beautiful as the work of a master composer, and that extends to all genres of music," he says. "It's been happening at Lee for a very long time. We're making a difference in the musical conversation of this generation because Lee placed such an emphasis on its importance, and thanks be to God that it's just become part of our DNA."

Service

The Gospel according to Matthew highlights a simple but profound theme of taking care of the least among us, and of the apostles taking the word of the Lord to far villages without any guarantee of their own most basic sustenance. That principle of a "cup of water in Jesus' name" forms the foundation of the Leonard Center at Lee University.

The program started in 2003 as a formulation of the "want to serve" that has existed since the first days of the university, according to Dr. William Lamb, director of the Leonard Center. Prior to Lee, Lamb was a school bus driver and a preacher who had started a backyard tutoring program, where college students went into the community to reach kids who otherwise wouldn't have access to support.

Lee President Paul Conn saw an opportunity to take Lamb's experience and passion and formally integrate it into the service mandate that has always been a component of the Lee experience.

"It helps our students recognize that it's a part of what God created us to be as a member of a community," Lamb says. "It sets the tone for their lives, personally and professionally. In the words of Dr. Conn, we can sing well, we can teach well, but we also need to serve well."

The Leonard Center, named in honor of legendary pastor Bill Leonard through a significant gift from Dr. John Gregory, reflects the spirit of "someone who cares."

It starts with Deke Day, the first weekend on campus for freshmen that sends 1,200 new students into the community to spend time with elderly people in dozens of nursing homes, and it continues through the Lee experience in programs that deliver hot meals to the hungry and lonely, tutor younger students who might otherwise be lost, provide financial counseling to those who can't afford it, or work with developmentally disabled children who need a friend.

Meaningful relationships are formed through weekly interactions, and new programs have started and flourished as a result of organic growth and expansion.

"Most of it has come through students who found a need and a way to address it, often discovering deficiencies through another service project," Lamb says.

Four core distinctives guide the Leonard Center's offerings: first-year programs like Deke Day; Global Perspectives, which marries service opportunities with Lee's study abroad requirement; service learning that integrates theory in practice, such as with accounting students and tax preparation assistance; and benevolence, the biblical basis that influences the reality that we all have a need to serve.

It's all cap-stoned with the Graduation Service Pledge, where students agree to leave Lee with a commitment to civic engagement, social justice, and professional work that reflects their values. Virtually 100 percent of Lee graduates have signed the pledge since it was introduced a decade ago.

"Not only do they serve throughout life, but they inspire others to do the same," Lamb explains.

Thousands of lives are touched by these campus programs, and many thousands more by the alumni who carry that mission forth. The Leonard Center has been recognized in the top three of more than 700 schools for its success with a service learning program – all rooted in that most basic of principles of taking care of "the least among us."

"The King will answer and say to them, 'Truly I say to you, to the extent that you did it to one of these brothers of Mine, even the least of them, you did it to Me.'"

Ray and Joan Conn (above) have helped envision, design, and build two dozen buildings on Lee's growing campus since 1988. The late Rich and Helen DeVos, shown at the 1998 dedication of the Helen DeVos College of Education, were the "lead donors" for numerous projects.

RICH & HELEN DEVOS — RAY & JOAN CONN:
Two Visionary Couples — One Wonderful Campus

Over the past three decades, the Lee University campus has emerged from its small core to a 125-acre campus which is widely admired for its beauty, functionality, and the creative consistency of basic architectural themes. As Lee has grown in enrollment and programs, it has created a campus to serve that growth.

Two couples, Ray and Joan Conn and Rich and Helen DeVos, have been the visionaries who have created this extraordinary physical campus. "More than any other individuals," says President Paul Conn, "these four people have had the long-term, sustained vision to make this campus such a lovely and effective collegiate setting."

Ray and Joan Conn are alums from the Classes of 1970 and '74. As the owner and CEO of Tri-Con, Inc., a general contracting company, and ArCon, Inc., an architectural design firm, Ray has participated in the creation of virtually every major structure on the Lee campus since 1989. More than just a typical design-build operation, the Conns have helped envision the larger aspects of campus development. It is Ray's creative, intelligent talent that gives Lee's campus the coherence which people see today.

The late Rich and Helen DeVos have been friends of Lee since the mid-1980s. They have led one of America's most successful business families from their home in Grand Rapids, Michigan. Beginning with a modest gift in 1988, and continuing with multiple seven-figure gifts until the present time, they have made a huge impact on the university. Their sustained commitment to the vision of a vibrant, growing campus has been one of the most remarkable parts of the Lee story.

"Look around you," President Conn says. "Wherever you look, you're seeing the fingerprints of Ray and Joan, and Rich and Helen. This simply would not have happened without them."

VISIONS *of* LEE UNIVERSITY

LIFT HIGH THE FLAME

LIFT HIGH THE FLAME

LIFT HIGH THE FLAME

VISIONS *of* LEE UNIVERSITY

91

LIFT HIGH THE FLAME

VISIONS *of* LEE UNIVERSITY

LIFT HIGH THE FLAME

104

LIFT HIGH THE FLAME

LIFT HIGH THE FLAME

LIFT HIGH THE FLAME

LIFT HIGH THE FLAME

LIFT HIGH THE FLAME

VISIONS *of* LEE UNIVERSITY

143